Seahorses

Black
Lawrence
Press

www.blacklawrence.com

Executive Editor: Diane Goettel
Book and Cover Design: Zoe Norvell
Cover Art: "Sea Horses" © 2019 John Francis, licensed by MGL, www.mglart.com

Published 2020 by Black Lawrence Press.
Printed in the United States.

for Arike
who never sleeps

Contents

1

2

3

Seahorses

1

Aubade

For children caged like hens –
Many without bread –

By the governor
And his promise of gold coins

For *fowls* caught
Near our town's doors –

The ones to blame
For the lack of jobs.

A morning song
For those pilloried on stage

With faces blue and *softened*
From rotten cabbage.

A mirror for the residents
Of this town

Whose laughter and applause
Crescendo

When each *fowl* goes limp
And is dragged off to *The Coop*

Where filth like him are held
For months at a time

Before being kicked
And kicked out

By *heroes* with guns
Protecting our town.

The Last Book

After it was tossed
Into the pyre

Husbands kissed
Their wives

For children
Parents bought

Toy authors
With dug out eyes

Cardinals
To Imams

At long last

Imams
To Cardinals

Al ham du li lah

As the flame rose
And glowed

Into the air
And night

The soot
Steady in climb

Cleansing sins
From wayward minds

God's will
In a new paradise

White Rooms

I think it's just us today
So I'll crank it halfway
But you have to scream
Like it's full voltage.
Deranged with pain
Is what the others say
And look for
When they rewind videos
To see who of the detained
First shuddered, screamed
Then passed out
In their own piss.
For both our sakes
Beg and scream.
Confess to all you didn't do
While foaming spit.
I remember camping
With your family
(Yes I have to fit the harness)
The steak and cold beers.
Julie thinks it's stupid
You should keep on like this
No wonder the twins
Have been taken from you
(The gag too)
And what about Laura
The shit she must put up with
The eye rolls and name calling
(I know you're in pain
But you're not doing it right
Your face must turn white

And please foam at the mouth)
Anyway Julie thinks it's stupid
What you're doing
For those god-forsaken people
Who don't even look
Or talk like you
Selfish not to put on the uniform
And defend the state like we do.
It kills me to do this.
Over shit immigrants
You don't even know?
When the guards return and ask
Tell them you've had a change of heart
And what shift you'd prefer.
Tell them your boot size
And colored baton you'd like to have.
Think of the twins. Think of Laura.

After Coming Home from The Detainment Camp

You take a long shower
With hot water

To cleanse yourself
Of the urine and stench

"Those foreign animals drink
And use to wash themselves."

You throw your uniform
Socks and underpants
In the washer

Then scrub your hands
A second time.

After dinner
You chat with your wife

About her favorite
Reality TV show –

Who among the characters
Wrestled each other to the ground

Who survived the night's
Elimination round.

You indulge your daughter
In a late-night snack
Of mint ice cream

Then tuck her in bed
After telling stories

Of monsters from far places
Who speak different languages
And are always filthy.

When the house is silent
You oil your gun

Polish your boots and baton
Test your walkies and
Arrange your keys.

And because you won't touch
Each *animal's* sweat and worms

In the morning, you'll buy
A new pair of latex gloves.

"But that's tomorrow"
You tell yourself

As you cradle two glasses
And a bottle of wine

For you and your loving wife
Who is waiting, naked
And impatient in bed.

Nooses

After they were discovered
At the local elementary school

The scandal broke
And made news.

To contain the conversation
And clarify his views

The Headmaster invited parents
That next morning

To the school
Where he held up nooses

And gently explained
That since no one
Was dangling from each

The ropes in his hands
Could not be nooses.

And, tightened around trees
Each is safe for playing Tarzan

If kids decide to swing
From branch to sandpit

Not to mention tug-of-war
When knotted on both ends
And the kids split into teams.

At the end of his speech
Across the room, tensions eased.

Parents thinking
Of withdrawing their kids

Went home with palettes
Of watercolor and nooses.

That evening, at kitchen tables
Throughout the district

Families were engrossed
In all manner of rope crafts –

Some painted them yellow
Some orange then pink

Some glued on plastic eyes
And right below
Painted fat lips

Some cared nothing
Of proportions

And placed them as chignon
On exotic Barbie dolls

Others, after dipping them
In purple dye

Laced them as scarves
Around the necks
Of toy gorillas.

William Tell

At recess
When the new kid –

A nine-year-old refugee
From a West African country –

Removed her pinafore
Unbuttoned her uniform
Stripped to her underskirt

Then stood by the wall
And placed the apple
On her head

The popular kids knew
She would join their group.

But they had to see
The initiation through.

After making her swear
She wouldn't tell anyone

They explained *slowly*
That it would only take five minutes

And instead of tiny stones –

A viable stand in for arrows
And a long-standing rule –

They'd use larger ones
Since she was African and taller
Than other girls in the group.

And it's the only way
A girl like her
Can be like them

But it was up to her
Since she wasn't being forced
To take part.

And so it was
That during recess
At the school in town

While teachers
Were chatting about sports
And eating burgers in the lounge

A nine-year-old refugee
From a West African country –

Stripped-down
To her underskirt –

Was being cheered
By a group of girls

Aiming stones
At an apple on her head

As the girl tried to
Swat each stone
And protect each gash

As blood trickled down
Her chin and neck

Her unformed breasts
Panties and underskirt.

Collateral Damage

In the orchards, the old revolutionaries
Have gathered again for tea

They meet at the general's house each morning
Below his balcony for tea cold unsweetened

Drunk from the same small cup
That's passed around after each slow sip

They say nothing about the passion
That gripped them in their youth

Nothing of the villages they cleansed with napalm
In the name of villages they fought for

They sit in silence for hours till it starts to get dark
Then one by one they stand and leave the yard

Saying nothing of the thousand infants
Whose burnt and severed heads

They counted and proudly hung on spikes
Whose teeth they wagered when playing cards

Infants who return to each revolutionary
After midnight, crawling on top each other

From the bedrooms all through the house
From the garden all through the compound

Infants hungry, crying, thinking the revolutionary
Their father, and his house the place of their birth

Mourning

I know those for whom
It's business.

A family trained
To thrash and wail

Roll on the ground
And rend attire

Who offer week-long seminars
And courses by the hour

On weeping for sibling
Parent or child

According to need
And what pockets allow.

The butcher, whose wife
Last night succumbed to fever

Has invited five mourners
To his house.

And on their way
The mourners talk about

The butcher's thick rug
And new divan

Flip coins on who should hold
The wife's yellowed hands

And what to charge the butcher
For extra hours.

They agree on songs to sing
Each wail's pitch

How long to stand against the wall
Arms folded, pensive

Before again heaving
Beating their breasts

Rolling on the floor
And breaking out in tears.

Calisthenics

A long
Evening walk

Around
The block.

Silence worn
As coat and
Top hat.

Sorrow tucked
In the left
Breast pocket.

The wind
Knotted gently
As necktie.

The Face You Wear

It's the lowered
Eyes

And demure
Smile

You've learned
To put on

As the sole
Black immigrant
On the cul-de-sac.

A face emptied
Of Lagos heat

Its clutter   noise
And busy spirit.

A face you know
Will put white neighbors
At ease

When you're outside
Mowing the lawn
Or raking leaves.

Vacant expressions
A constant smile

A slow nod and pause
That says

Spit on my head
I'll wipe drool
From your mouth.

A face arranged
To calmly look on

When one neighbor deposits
Shit in your mailbox

A steaming pile
Beside your door

Or when another
Walks over

To complain again
Of loud immigrants

With their Ebola
And lice.

Unlike you
This quiet immigrant
With lowered eyes

Who mows his lawn
And rakes his yard.

The kind this neighbor
Wouldn't mind
Having over for dinner.

A good immigrant
Whose demure smile

Signals nothing
Of the old city within him –

Its proud people
Its long history.

A face put on each morning
That reads

Squat over me and shit
I'll laugh with you
As you're doing it

2

Before Dawn with Angel Raziel

You bathe with loofahs
Soaked in papaya juice

And delight
In gently draping cloth
Over laughter

Watching it swell
With light

Then peeling it off
And wrapping it

On your heads
As turbans.

And after sowing roses
In his suit's seam

You sit still
As he dips jasmines
In yellow

And swirls them
For hours

Across your eyelids

Until somewhere
In your soul

Pupils untrained
In music

Lift French horns
And play adagio.

Moons
Beside themselves

Lie beside oxen
Naked.

Bees talk dirty
To poplar trees.

Husbands
For their wives
Model chemise.

And notes –
Long erased
From the heart –

Line back in scale
And slowly rise

Like newly released
Lanterns

Floating upward
In the eastern sky.

Revelations

On the day and time
Of the passing of man

Pots and kettles
Will reconcile

Each will welcome
The other's black

From the same gourd
They'll drink wine

And from the same bowl
They'll eat yams

Feeding each other gently
In soft stewed mounds

♦

Hens will borrow the moon's abacus
And take it to the coop

But just because
They borrow its abacus

Doesn't mean
They'll sing of the moon

They'll pull the beads
And sing instead

Of raised and feathered necks
Breeze beneath the cypress

And of love between gators
Octopi and ferrets –

Those gained and others
Unrequited

♦

Goats will get drunk
On beer carefully brewed

To turn cheeks red
Or gently rouge

And warm from days
Of song and drink

Mugs raised
To nanny-goats

In blouse
And skirts trimmed

They'll raise their legs
In beat and rhyme

To tunes that echoed
From old men's hearts

On the day and time
Of the passing of man

Jesus' Day Job

Before the beatitudes
And disciples

The healings, the cross
And testaments
Of his faithful

He worked in a shop
On the outskirts
Of Capernaum

A boat maker
Who daily carved up beams
And raised scaffolding

In the ribs of boats
From dawn till evening

With carpenters
Who came to work
Drunk on spirits

And laughed
Through slurred tales

Of ruined trysts
And pulled down
Panties.

Each day
At close of day

He sweeps the sod
And sawdust

Into a pile
In the corner
Of the shop

Laughing again
At the thought
Of his co-workers

Who never push plank
Or raise hammer

Who will return
Tomorrow, again
Drunk

To find their skiffs
Built and leaned
Against the wall

Not once concerned
About the miracle
Of how each gets done

But full of stories
Of wages lost
And women of the night

Glorious breasts
And barrels of wine.

The Good and Pure

Leave it to the good and pure
To ruin the fun for the rest of us
Happy to swap stories and pictures
Of our times in Sodom, after fondling
Each other's crotch by the famous
Statue of men and dogs embraced
In lust. Stories of women drunk
And drinking from the same glass.
Pictures with a would-be-bride and
Her retinue of virgin friends in white
Each holding a large pink dildo
And a note saying "for her other man".
The good and pure, with their grave looks
And long cassocks, who show up
Outside the city's gates to wipe vomit
From each drunk's face. Wash his clothes
When he defecates. When all we want
Is to see him stagger, fall on his face.
Give him more to drink, then fornicate.
Now they camp outside Sodom –
The good and pure – in numbers.
Raising placards. Warning pilgrims
Thirsting for delight to turn back
Because they've read the signs
That god's wrath is upon us
And it will leave this city
Burned down to ash.

Standing in the Ruins
of Gomorrah

Here
A house stood

Where widows
Begged alms

Shared bread
And kissed at night.

Here
A prophet
Sat with prostitutes

And of the little
They gave

He drank with joy
And ate.

Beside these walls
A drunk rose from stupor
Pushed aside bottles

Swearing god spoke
And he'd heard the call.

And here –

The night before
This town was
Burnt down –

My father broke fruit
With the same brother

That for years
Took his wife.

Those Sore of Soul

Deal gently
With those
Sore of Soul

For whom
Each invitation

Or word spoken
Is wound to sea-salt

Or boil
Cut open.

Forgive
Their furrowed brows
And punch of air

Their voice
A treble loud

And their swell
Of chest

Whose welts –

Thick and reddened
For years –

Must be softly licked
And pressed

Till they thaw
Give off pus
And slowly clear

And the seahorses
Long buried within

Over time
Begin to reveal
Themselves.

West of Neverland

After years of working
West of Neverland

In the most unsanitary
Meatpacking company

And living in a tenement
Overrun by mice

Hook took by foot
The same route

Peter, Wendy, John
And Michael flew

When they soared
Straight on till morning

After passing the second star
On the right.

He returned home
To Neverland

With gray beard
And rusting hook

Gaunt, bald
Sunken-eyed

With worms, lice
And a distant look.

He returned
To find Smee gone.

His pirates
The lost boys

Croc
And the ticking clock.

Looking across
Marooner's Rock

He sighs
From remorse

For what started as a game
And how it went all wrong.

How he agreed

(Now removing his shoes
And stilts)

To play the grown up

(His coat, beard
And wooden teeth)

Who held children prisoners
After chasing them
Like dogs.

How he bludgeoned Wendy
And broke her arms

Tied John and Michael
For days

Till they begged
To eat rats.

And Tiger Lilly
Tiger Lilly...

It was a part
He played too well

One he's now
Resigned to

As he slowly adjusts
And reties the stilts

Slips on the coat
And pushes down
His wooden teeth

Again becoming
The aged man

From the meatpacking
Company

The one diseased
With worms and lice

Who must return to work
After daybreak

Before the ticking clock
Strikes nine.

Samson

If you understood
How the soil within him
Was seedless and dry

How its sole tree
Gnarled and wound
Bent far from its spine

How branches raised in the wind
Cracked   then fell
On the ground of his heart

You wouldn't speak
Of just his strength
His hair or Delilah

The Person You Once Were

Taking down this picture
Of the person you once were

And smashing it against the wall
Of your blue and brown house

Won't change opinions of you
Held by those you've wronged

Who still call you a sloth
And a shameless drunk.

This was twenty years ago, when
The person you once were

Never showed up to work
Gambled wages held in his trust

Drank through the night
And wrote others off.

Smashing this picture
Against the wall

Won't signal to those you've wronged
The bitter work you've done –

The nights alone shaking
From cold sweat.

Days before therapists
When you broke down and wept.

Let this picture be a reminder
Of the years you've spent
Moving the dial

Toward the person you now are
Able to lie through the night
With its blue and white song

Able to rise before dawn
Pick up the hoe and cutlass
And go in search of work.

The Emerald City

Just because you know
It's within

Doesn't mean
You should call those

In search of it
Foolish.

Like the young man
You're talking about

Who left his wife
And child

A six-figure salary
And a big house –

With a games room
And a large unfenced yard –

To pursue his dream
Of basket weaving

Even when we all knew
It wouldn't pan out.

So what
If this man's
Yellow brick road

Is not yellow
And is no road

But –

And pardon
The forced
Metaphor –

A boat
Months at sea
Low on supplies

With an oarsman
Weakened from heat

Lost on the horizon
Yet holding out hope

For fresh wind
To again swell
The masts

As he continues
Toward that city

We all know
He won't find.

3

When Lights Go Out in the Village

And the watchman
Tired from patrols
Leans on the gates

I find myself awake
In the same dream

Of goats painting
Their hooves green.

Of women, drunk
On the aroma
Of bell peppers

Passed out
In the village square
Naked.

Of my father again
In the family shrine

Crossing himself
Then reciting

Bismillah

Hoping the floating boat
That ferries the dead
Passes by

Without dropping anchor
Outside my house.

Sometimes, The Way It Is

"You don't ever let go of the thread."
— WILLIAM STAFFORD

You can.

Not forever
But for a while

To stay
In the hospital

For days
With a child

Plagued
By an illness

That has
Left her gaunt

And robbed
Of speech

For which
Tests are done

But reveal
Nothing.

You sit beside her
Tonight

Knowing
In the back
Of your mind

That metaphors
Will not suffice.

That there's nothing fancy
About it to trace

Until you arrive
At insight.

Only this –

A child held
And threaded
With tubes

The hard thought
Of how long

To let all
The machines hum

The eventual silence
With its red cloth

And the mornings
Before dawn

When you try to fill
The child's non-voice

With your failed
And lumbering songs.

Threnody

for Modupe Doherty

> "If dirges and planned lamentations
> Could put off death,
> Men would be singing for ever."
> — SOPHOCLES

I.

Saturday mornings
Will never
Be the same.

II.

Whistle of kettle atop a stove
Is no more.
The teacup is dry.

III.

No hands butter the bread.
None pass the jam.
Chairs of the dinner table collect dust.
Plates remain empty.

And They Called Him Cain

Let's not sour our hearts
At this child

Whose father borrowed
A stereo from an aunt

Pulled and dusted a coat
From bent rack

Shined holed shoes
Despite cracks
Then washed, dried

And starched his only shirt
Before inviting us

To his house.

For now, let's make
No comparison

To another, whose name
He shares

And pay no heed
To priests

Who, after casting beads
Say to relatives –

"This child will waylay travelers
And in time, his parents at night.

He'll hold his mother under a knife
Till she puts her last necklace in his bag."

For now, let's nod
Gently to the father's music

Dance
When he dances

Tease on neighbors
Having twins

And him
Just one baby.

Let's eat the little cooked
From his small means –

The cold rice and stew he offered
As we came in.

Let's raise our cups
To his wife

Sing her health
And before leaving

Hold this newborn
To our chests
And wish him strength

Before putting him back
On the grime-soaked bed.

Pulling Weeds

Not the tired thought
Of thistle and thorn

As metaphors
For lost loves

That when cleared
Allow a glimpse

Into how
The aching heart
Leans

When pried
From the pull and clutch

Of a past now lost
And wounds quietly borne

Nor discourse
On the virtue of distant ideas

Artfully held or
Carelessly joined

No dressed-up language
In heels and lace

For the gratitude
You feel today

Despite the clot
And dialysis

Months-long spasm
And throbbing knees

To again, from the waist
Yank each staggered weed

Tossed in a pile you'll dump
At the public works
West of the city

Gratitude this evening
For the brown mulch
Beneath your feet

The rest and rustle
Of light and wind

Upon the thick green bush
And frail thin trees

Gratitude
For the wide staccatos
Of croaking frogs

The burrow and buzz
Of mice and bees

Winning the Lottery

Unlike the U.S. where winners
Pose behind large cardboard checks

Have their names mentioned on television
And who at work inform their friends

Here, it's better to stay lukewarm
When news of your winnings come

And you realize once and for all
You'll never again be poor
And from now can eat as you want.

Instead of dashing out and buying
Designer shoes, a first-class cruise

Or driving through untarred roads
In your new air-conditioned vehicle

It's better to keep living as you do
In that two-room bungalow

You share with three uncles, an aunt
And five nephews, with whom

You queue each morning for hours
Waiting turns to fetch water
From the house's sole running tap.

And when power goes out
Don't run to buy generators

To draw light into the kitchen
The hall, the front and side yards.

Better to remain as you are. Indifferent
To the lack of power again tonight

Like those uncles and aunt, whom
You've looked on for years askance
Themselves lottery winners

Who gave away boats, shoes, cars
And chose to live in a commune
Far from town, who –

Even now, as you sort through
Your new statement of account –

Are sitting outside, loud
With conversation and laughter

Wiping sweat with soaked blouse
Peeling leaves from corn meals
Shared by the moon's light.

Communion

After years of talking over each other
We can finally sit on this porch

Unmoored from the sullenness
We've grown accustomed.

How I don't guffaw with scorn
At you going door to door

Sharing what to you are keys
Of a yearned-for kingdom.

How you don't roll your eyes
At my lengthy treatise

On Milton's *Lycidas* and
Paraphrased psalms –

Better, I held
Than anything offered

In those pamphlets
With smiling faces

You leave with those
I call gullible
But you call believers.

How in this July heat
We line bagels with cream cheese

Slice cheddar and tomatoes
Cut carrots and pour iced tea.

Not unlike rowers
Paddling in opposite directions
For years on the same ship

Who pause from time to time
To share a simple meal
Of stale bread and salted fish

Before leaning over the prow
To contemplate the low clouds

The red sun and the gulls
Framed in its sinking light

Who after drinking
From the same dented
Rusting container

Won't acquiesce on where
Or how to steer the ship

Just as you won't say I'm right
And I won't share your beliefs

Have a change of heart
And call this evening meal
What it never was and is.

Monasteries

Count them lucky
Who have them within

Who feel no need
To follow prophets

To distant islands
Or remote beaches

Where salvation is assured
And paradise promised

Who, seated as they are
Remain beside altars

Where *blue* and *green*
Sing arias.

In them, Night
With a thousand yellow lights
Braids its hair

And bathes with waters
From dark village wells.

A Good Ending

There's a place
For good endings

Where parting
Yields enough music

To keep
Each person
Steady

Through its wide
And fading
Harmonic

As when an eraser
Is taken

To the dot
And curve

Of the fermata
On *e*

And the notes
And lines
Of the music sheet

Are slowly
Rubbed clean

Leaving
Impressions

Of songs many
Will not hear

And few
Considered music

Old Friends

Give thanks
That they were once here

That for a time
They were regular players

In the low-grade production
Difficult for you to accept
Is no longer there

Which explains why
You still wear

Your gold magician's robe
And blue dunce hat

Drink from pink gourds
Before calling forth
Sprites.

Gone is the chorus that
Cheered each drink
And dance of spirit.

Gone the nightly rituals
Of failed arrangements
In prop and rhyme.

Let each burned out light
Be a sign of gratitude
That you were once together

All bad actors
In a poorly produced play

Attended by no one
On this abandoned stage.

Acknowledgments

Many thanks to the journals where the following poems first appeared in their early or final forms.

And They Called Him Cain: *Bramble*. Monasteries. Those Sore of Soul: *Brain Mill Press Online*. Calisthenics. Samson: *Comstock Review*. Mourning: *Foglifter*. When Lights Go Out in the Village: *Poetry Ireland Review*. The Person You Once Were. West of Neverland: *Plane Tree*. Pulling Weeds: *Poetry South*. Standing in the Ruins of Gomorrah: *Ruminate Magazine*. Revelations: *The Drunken Boat*. Before Dawn with Angel Raziel: *TriQuarterly*.

Special thanks also to David Shumate. Kim Stafford. Megan Merchant. Tara DaPra. Christina Kubasta. Susan Tolbert. Brian Sutton. Joseph Harrington. Karla Huston. Folabo Ajayi. Diane Goettel. Angela Leroux-Lindsey. Black Lawrence Press. And of course, Emily.

ABAYOMI ANIMASHAUN is the author of three poetry collections and editor of three anthologies. A winner of the Hudson Prize and a recipient of a grant from the International Center for Writing and Translation, Animashaun teaches at the University of Wisconsin, Oshkosh and lives in Green Bay, Wisconsin.